GEARED FOR GROWTH BIBLE STUDIES

OUR MAGNIFICENT GOD

A STUDY IN ISAIAH

BIBLE STUDIES TO IMPACT THE LIVES OF ORDINARY PEOPLE

Written by John Priddle

The Word Worldwide

CHRISTIAN FOCUS

Christian Focus Publications

publishes books for all ages

Our mission statement –

STAYING FAITHFUL

In dependence upon God we seek to help make His infallible word, the Bible, relevant. Our aim is to ensure that the Lord Jesus Christ is presented as the only hope to obtain forgiveness of sin, live a useful life and look forward to heaven with Him.

REACHING OUT

Christ's last command requires us to reach out to our world with His gospel. We seek to help fulfill that by publishing books that point people towards Jesus and help them develop a Christ-like maturity. We aim to equip all levels of readers for life, work, ministry and mission.

Books in our adult range are published in three imprints.
Christian Focus contains popular works including biographies, commentaries, basic doctrine, and Christian living. Our children's books are also published in this imprint.
Mentor focuses on books written at a level suitable for Bible College and seminary students, pastors, and other serious readers; the imprint includes commentaries, doctrinal studies, examination of current issues, and church history.
Christian Heritage contains classic writings from the past.

For details of our titles visit us on our website
www.christianfocus.com

ISBN 1-85792-909-8

Copyright © WEC International

Published in 2003 by
Christian Focus Publications, Geanies House,
Fearn, Ross-shire, IV20 ITW, Scotland
and
WEC International, Bulstrode, Oxford Road,
Gerrards Cross, Bucks, SL9 8SZ

Cover design by Alister MacInnes

Printed and bound by J W Arrowsmith, Bristol

CONTENTS

QUESTIONS AND NOTES

ANSWER GUIDE

STUDY 1

QUESTIONS

DAY 1 *Isaiah 40:1-5; Matthew 3:1-3.*
a) What message of comfort was to be spoken to God's people (v. 2)?
b) Who does Matthew identify as the 'voice' of verse 3? What kind of preparation did he advocate for the coming of God?
c) What guarantee lay behind God's promise of a coming glory (v. 5)?

DAY 2 *Isaiah 40:6-11.*
a) What joyful message was to be proclaimed?
b) How is God and man compared here?

DAY 3 *Isaiah 40:12-17.*
a) What do these verses reveal about God?
b) Why are nations no threat to God?

DAY 4 *Isaiah 40:18-26.*
a) Where should the people look in order to gain some idea of God's greatness?
b) How is idol worship shown to be foolish?

DAY 5 *Isaiah 40:27-31.*
a) What had been the complaint of the people (v. 27)?
b) How does God answer them in verse 28?
c) What great promises are given here to all who trust in God?

DAY 6 *Isaiah 41:1-4.*
A human deliverer is promised. Who motivates and enables this deliverer to help Israel?

DAY 7 *Isaiah 41:5-10.*
a) How was Israel to react to the rise of this superpower? Why would it be possible to react like this?
b) How would the nations react?

NOTES

If Isaiah anticipates the day when the people would receive the joyful news of their release from captivity, he is also anticipating many themes which appear in the New Testament. Just as Israel was far from her homeland so we as sinners are held captive by Satan, obliged to follow his dictates and unable to break free (Eph. 2:1-3).

Matthew identifies John the Baptist as fulfilling the prophecy of Isaiah 40:3. His ministry heralded the coming of the Lord Jesus. The Greek translation of the Old Testament (the 'Septuagint Version', often written as LXX) translates the 'good tidings' of verse 9 by a word which has a deep meaning in the New Testament – 'gospel', or 'good news'. Jesus came 'proclaiming the good news of God' (Mark 1:14). He came to save us from our sins (Matt. 1:21) and this message is to be carried to all with every bit of enthusiasm as the announcement of the nation's release from Babylon would be.

Several contrasts mentioned here are developed in succeeding chapters. Notice the contrast between God and idols and between God and men. The comparison between God and idols is one of Isaiah's favourite themes running through this book. What rich pictures of God we have! Spend time contemplating on who God says He is: Eternal, Self-existing, Creator, All-knowing and All-powerful. How unreasonable to think that we should put our trust in someone or something else. Viewed from God's perspective, men's earthly kingdoms are easily swept away (40:24). Nothing happens by accident. God uses the events of contemporary history to bring about His will. Just as Cyrus was raised up to release His people, so later God would use the events of Roman history to bring Joseph and Mary to Bethlehem for the birth of the Lord Jesus Christ.

God promises strength to the weary and His promises can be trusted. God is great and we are not to forget this. Our responsibility is to wait or hope in the Lord. If we focus on our problems we will get depressed while focusing on the Lord Jesus will give renewed confidence (Heb. 12:1-3). Psalm 37 exhorts us to 'trust' in the Lord, 'commit' our way to Him and be 'still' before Him (vv. 3, 5, 7). God was calling His people to do this despite turmoil in the nations surrounding them. The future need not be scary for those who trust in God.

STUDY 2

QUESTIONS

DAY 1 *Isaiah 41:8-16.*
a) What were the people called not to do?
b) What promises were they given?
c) How would they respond to eventual victory (v. 16)?

DAY 2 *Isaiah 41:17-24.*
a) How did God illustrate His abundant provision for those who seek Him in their need?
b) What characteristic of God sets Him apart here from idols?

DAY 3 *Isaiah 41:25-29.*
a) What brings about the silence of the idols verse 28?
b) Can you think of any notable examples in the Bible where only God could interpret dreams concerning the future?

DAY 4 *Isaiah 42:1-4.*
What are we told about the Servant here that points forward to Jesus (Matt. 3:16, 17; 12:18-21; 17:5)?

DAY 5 *Isaiah 42:5-9.*
a) What are we reminded about God in verse 5?
b) What commission is given to the Servant here?

DAY 6 *Isaiah 42:10-17.*
a) What reaction is to follow the unveiling of the Servant's ministry?
b) What do the contrasting pictures of verses 13 and 16 show us of God's character?

DAY 7 *Isaiah 42:18-25*
a) What differences are there between the servant here (probably Israel) and the Servant of earlier verses?
b) What explanation is given for the nation's plight?

NOTES

How do we react to the daily news broadcasts? What if a new superpower or terror group were suddenly to emerge? Isaiah has announced the arrival of one (Cyrus) and anticipates the panic and reaction of the nations (41:5-8): a frantic effort to construct more idols. God pours scorn on this approach as idols are described as dumb, inanimate objects, unable to help (41:22-24). On what are we relying? Astrology is big business today as people wonder about their future, and yet it is condemned by God.

Instead of resorting to panic, God's people are told not to fear. Sometimes there is a gap between our heads and hearts. We might know a truth with our minds but our emotions cannot encompass it. God declares Himself to be on their side ready to help, strengthen and uphold them (41:10). Paul could say, 'I can do everything through him who gives me strength' (Phil. 4:13). Joseph and Moses both enjoyed God's presence (Gen. 39:2; Exod. 33:14). Jesus promised His disciples, 'And surely I am with you always, to the very end of the age' (Matt. 28:20). God's friendship outlasts all others. His friendship gives satisfaction because it penetrates to the depth of our spirit nature.

God said that their enemies would ultimately disappear (41:11, 12). These words of ultimate victory remind us of the words of Jesus: 'I will build my church, and the gates of Hades will not overcome it' (Matt. 16:18). The church has faced many difficulties throughout its history but like the Jewish nation it still lives on! When we are on God's side we are on the victory side. Be encouraged even if currently you appear to be struggling in the battle.

God responds to those who are poor and needy (41:17). The widow in Luke 18 is held up as an encouragement to pray as her request was granted. The tax collector rather than the proud Pharisee went home justified (Luke 18:9-14) as he had confessed his need. Spiritually speaking the ground is desert around us. Let us ask God for water to refresh us and those around us. God's concern is that He will get all the glory (41:20). Those who truly belong to God can rely on Him to uphold and strengthen them even in the midst of troubles. Are we panicking or trusting?

GOD'S SERVANT (42:1-9)
Did Isaiah's hearers have any idea who this Servant would be? Probably not. The only One who could be equal to this ministry of bringing justice and spiritual enlightenment to the world is Jesus Christ. Think about His character. We have a clearer picture of it than ever Isaiah could have had because we look back to the cross. His gentleness rebukes our brashness and His faithfulness rebukes our carelessness. Let us remember that His attitude is to be ours (Phil. 2:5-8). Remember, His universal concerns should be ours too. Missionary interest didn't begin in Acts; it was always in the heart and mind of God.

STUDY 3

CREATOR AND REDEEMER

QUESTIONS

DAY 1 *Isaiah 43:1-7.*
a) Why are the people told not to fear?
b) What has been the cost of redemption for us (Matt. 20:28; Eph. 1:7)?

DAY 2 *Isaiah 43:8-13.*
a) To what would the nation of Israel bear witness?
b) To what does the church bear witness today (Eph. 3:10)?

DAY 3 *Isaiah 43:14-28.*
a) What were the people being reminded about in verses 16, 17? What are they encouraged to do now (vv. 18, 19)?
b) What great promise is given to those who respond to God (v. 25)?

DAY 4 *Isaiah 44:1-5.*
a) What would be the effect of God's blessing given to His people?
b) Discuss briefly the effect of the coming of the Holy Spirit at Pentecost
(Acts 2:1-4, 14, 37, 41).

DAY 5 *Isaiah 44:6-20.*
a) What titles does God give Himself here?
b) What always lies behind false worship (vv. 9, 18, 19; Romans 1:21, 22)?

DAY 6 *Isaiah 44:21-23.*
What is the cause for celebration here?

DAY 7 *Isaiah 44:24-28.*
a) List some of the things God has done, does and promises to do?
b) Who is identified as the human deliverer for Israel?

NOTES

God is Israel's Redeemer. This title of God appears thirteen times in chapters 40-66. In the Old Testament, property, animals, persons and the nation were all 'redeemed' by the payment of a price. Somebody paid the price necessary to free property from mortgage, animals from slaughter, and persons from slavery, even death. The story of Ruth (Ruth 3, 4) illustrates the duty of a 'kinsman redeemer' to buy back a property which had been lost to the family. Redemption is more than mere deliverance. It focuses on a price paid to let the condemned go free. *The New Bible Dictionary* (Inter-Varsity Press, p. 1079) makes this statement about the use of this word in the Old Testament: 'Where redemption occurs there is the thought of effort. Yahweh redeems "with a stretched out arm". He makes known His strength. Because he loves His people He redeems them at cost to Himself. His effort is regarded as the "price".' Redemption is very much a New Testament word. Jesus 'did not come to be served, but to serve, and to give his life as a ransom for many' (Mark 10:45). Redemption focuses in on our plight as sinners and the need for a ransom payment to set us free. The price paid was the blood of Jesus (1 Pet. 1:18, 19).

Spiritual blindness leads to idol worship. God exposes and condemns their self-delusion. But are we any better? Paul was commissioned to go to the Gentiles to 'open their eyes and turn them from darkness to light, and from the power of Satan to God' (Acts 26:18). He could later write: 'The god of this age has blinded the minds of unbelievers, so that they cannot see the light of the gospel of the glory of Christ' (2 Cor. 4:4). Only the Bible can 'make us wise for salvation in Christ Jesus (2 Tim. 3:15-17).

If chapter 42 ends with God judging His people, the 'But' of 43:1 would remind them again of His unfailing care for them. Waters, rivers and fire speak of difficult things that happen to us in the Christian life. It is not *if* they come but *when*. It is taken for granted that the grace of God does not carry us to the skies on 'flowery beds of ease'. There will be temptations and trials as long as we live but God will be with us.

Israel was a living proof of the existence of God. Their continued existence and return from captivity was testimony to God's intervention on their behalf. No idol could have done this. God described them as 'people formed for myself that they may proclaim my praise' (43:21). Privilege and responsibility! Peter wrote to believers saying they were 'a chosen people ... that you may declare the praises of him who called you out of darkness into his wonderful light' (1 Pet. 2:9). Every believer is a witness to God's grace and goodness; God's 'manifold wisdom' is seen in the church (Eph. 3:10). What are our lives revealing about God to those around us?

STUDY 4

ONLY ONE SAVIOUR

QUESTIONS

DAY 1 *Isaiah 45:1-7.*
a) What does God promise to do for Cyrus?
b) Why will God do all this?

DAY 2 *Isaiah 45:8-10.*
Why is it foolish to try and oppose God (Isa. 29:16; Rom. 9:19-21)?

DAY 3 *Isaiah 45:11-19.*
a) What will Cyrus be led to do for Israel (Ezra 1:1-4)?
b) What truth will other nations discover about God (vv. 14, 18b)?

DAY 4 *Isaiah 45:20-25.*
a) What universal command is given in verse 22? Why should this be obeyed?
b) What additional claim does God make in verse 23b? In what context does Paul quote this verse in Romans 14:9-13?

DAY 5 *Isaiah 46:1-7.*
a) What great differences between God and idols are highlighted here?
b) How does 1 Kings 18:25-29 illustrate the truth of verse 7?

DAY 6 *Isaiah 46:8-13.*
a) What picturesque description is given of Cyrus in verse 11?
b) What impresses you most about God in these verses?

DAY 7 *Isaiah 47.*
a) What qualities of God had Babylon taken upon herself in her pride (vv. 7, 8, 10)?
b) What warnings against occultic practices, including astrology, should we be taking note of here?

NOTES

Cyrus, born of royal parents, came to the throne about 559 BC in a small Persian kingdom called Ansham. In 549 BC he conquered the Median king, Astyages, his overlord and his mother's father. With the Medes and Persians now unified into a single force, he conquered the kingdom of Lydia in 547 BC and later Babylon in 539 BC. He surprised Babylon by diverting the river and entering the city along the dried-up river bed. References to Cyrus are found in Daniel (Dan. 1:21; 2:39; 7:5; 10:1) and also in secular history. The opening chapters of Ezra contain Cyrus' proclamation allowing the Jews to return to their homeland.

It is important to remember that Isaiah is predicting the events surrounding Cyrus many years (at least 150) in advance of them actually happening. In fact, Jerusalem was still standing and yet to be destroyed. There is no reason to suppose that Isaiah 45 is a description of events after they have taken place. One good reason for trusting the Bible is the number of predictions in it which have been accurately fulfilled. Of special note are the many prophecies fulfilled concerning the birth, life, death and resurrection of our Lord Jesus. What God says about the future will come to pass.

Though Cyrus is mentioned, he is not prominent in these chapters. God is. He is unique. Down through the ages idolatry has challenged this uniqueness of God but it is God who initiates and ensures victory for His people. He raised up Cyrus and deposed Babylon. He alone is the God who gives salvation and urges us to turn to Him for it (Isa. 45:22). Is He your God and Saviour?

While God disciplines His people, He also is the 'Good Shepherd' who cares for them. Isaiah 46:3,4 is an eloquent testimony to this. From conception to old age God said He was with them; He took an active interest in their welfare, ensuring continual help and deliverance. God is still the same today. Romans 8:28-39 is a very moving summary of God's care for His people today: 'in all things God works for the good of those who love him ... If God is for us who can be against us ...'.

STUDY 5

QUESTIONS

DAY 1 *Isaiah 48:1-11.*
a) What failure on Israel's part is dealt with in verses 3-6a?
b) How were the people to understand the hard things that were happening to them (vv. 9-11).

DAY 2 *Isaiah 48:12-22.*
a) What particular prophecy is stated here as a challenge to those who worship idols?
b) What incentive is there in these verses to put God first in our lives?

DAY 3 *Isaiah 49:1-7.*
a) Which statement in this passage has a parallel in John 1:11; Matthew 27:20-26. What did God say would happen?
b) What had God done to prepare His Servant for all of this?

DAY 4 *Isaiah 49:8-21.*
a) What two pictures does the Lord give of Himself to denote His care for His people (vv. 10, 15)?
b) In quoting verse 8 in 2 Corinthians 6:2, what warning does Paul add?

DAY 5 *Isaiah 49:22–50:3.*
a) In Isaiah 13:2 the Lord promises to raise His banner to bring about the destruction of Babylon. What is the purpose of the same action in verse 22?
b) What reason is given for the present plight of the nation (50:1)?

DAY 6 *Isaiah 50:4-7.*
What further parallels exist between the Speaker here and the Lord Jesus in Matthew 11:28; John 8:29; Luke 22:63? What conclusion can we draw?

DAY 7 *Isaiah 50:8-11.*
a) Why is the Servant so confident in spite of all His suffering (vv. 8, 9)?
What confidence can Christians have today (Rom. 8:31-35)?
b) What is the difference between the people described in verses 10, 11?

NOTES

There are at least six references to listening in this section (Isa. 48:1, 12, 14; 49:1; 50:4). God, in refusing to give up in His actions towards Israel of Isaiah's time, calls on them to listen. Do we take time to really listen to God? Had the nation listened they would have avoided a lot of unnecessary pain and suffering. In a clear prophetic reference to the Lord Jesus we are told that He listened 'like one being taught' (Isa. 50:4). Listening to and obeying God, just as Jesus experienced, may still bring suffering, but God is there to help even in these dark moments.

In chapter 48 God calls on His people to live up to their claim to be His people. He reminds them of things He has told them in advance, through His prophets, and says He is going to do the same thing now so that they will again be able to see how powerful He is. God speaks of their affliction as refining for service. This principle is still valid today (Heb. 12:11; 1 Pet. 1:6, 7).

Paul quite clearly takes the message of salvation here (Isa. 49:8) as applying to the Gospel era (2 Cor. 6:2) and so alongside the call to Israel to come back to Jerusalem there is the preparation for this same call to go to all nations. Now is the time to seek the Lord.

God returns to the problem of their suffering in chapter 50. They are suffering not because God has deserted them but because they have deserted Him. The Servant again comes to light. There are four 'Servant Songs' in Isaiah: 42:1-7; 49:1-6; 50:4-9; 52:13–53:12. In thought and teaching they are linked more closely with the New Testament than any other Old Testament scriptures. Who is this Servant who does such a work of great importance? This figure certainly finds its fulfilment in Jesus Christ. It may well be that as the prophet began his theme he was identifying it with his own rejection by the people. Certainly the challenge at the end of Isaiah 50 seems to fit in with the prophet's own day and this is what we would expect. Isaiah must write for his own contemporaries even as he was given these fleeting glances of God's plan for the future salvation of all nations.

STUDY 6

QUESTIONS

DAY 1 *Isaiah 51:1-8.*
a) What historical fact are the Israelites told to remember? How would this help them?
b) Who were told not to fear (v. 7)? What did God promise them?

DAY 2 *Isaiah 51:7-11.*
a) What did the people want God to do?
b) What were they confident of?

DAY 3 *Isaiah 51:12-16.*
a) How does God seek to alleviate any fears the people might have had?
b) Discuss how fear of others could affect our relationship with God.

DAY 4 *Isaiah 51:17-23.*
a) What figure of speech is used in connection with the punishment of Jerusalem and her inhabitants?
b) Matthew 26:36-39, 42 has the same idea in a New Testament setting. What did God do for His people that He did not do for His Son (Isa. 51:22)? Why was this?

DAY 5 *Isaiah 52:1-12.*
a) Who is to be given praise for Jerusalem's deliverance?
b) Compare Romans 10:14, 15 with verse 7. What Good News is to be carried to the world today?
c) What warning is given in verse 11? In what connection does Paul quote this verse in 2 Corinthians 6:14-18?

DAY 6 *Isaiah 52:13-15.*
In this introduction to the great 53rd chapter of Isaiah, what two contrasting pictures are we given of the Servant (obviously referring to the Lord Jesus).

QUESTIONS (contd.)

DAY 7 *Isaiah 53.1-12*

　　a) What type of sufferings are referred to? How did Jesus react to them (I Pet. 2:23)?

　　b) Why did the Lord Jesus endure all this suffering?

　　c) What references are there to His resurrection?

No wonder some of the most majestic anthems written have found their inspiration in these chapters! Constantly our thoughts jump from the historical incidents to the life and death of Jesus, encapsulating as it does salvation for all mankind.

Chapter 51 hints that Jerusalem's suffering has been immense. Subject to the taunts of her oppressors she is facing famine and possible extinction. But God is not finished with His people. In their hour of need God comes with a revelation of who He is and gives them hope for the future. God was watching over His people even in a faraway land. He was stirring up a righteous remnant (51:1, 9) to call upon Him. We might imagine that everyone would jump at the call to move out of Babylon and return to Jerusalem, yet for many, Babylon was probably quite comfortable; certainly much more comfortable than returning across hundreds of miles of desert to a ruined city that would require to be built. How apt then that they should be reminded of Abraham. God promises His help and that with His help they will return with singing.

God called the people too to action (52:1, 2). They were to appropriate what God would make possible for them. They were called to 'sit enthroned' and 'free' themselves from the chains on their necks. Christians have been raised up and seated with Christ in the heavenly realms and we are to exercise authority in the name of the Lord Jesus. God has given us weapons to overcome Satan. Satan would like to keep us in bondage with negative thoughts, doubts about our salvation. 'They overcame him by the blood of the Lamb and by the word of their testimony' (Rev. 12:11).

The greatest of all the Servant passages (Isa. 53) now comes in the midst of the call to come out of Babylon and to rebuild Jerusalem. The fact is nobody can possibly fill this role but the Lord Jesus Christ in His earthly life, atoning death and triumphant resurrection. So we need to see beyond the story of the simple deliverance of God's people from bondage in Babylon to the redemption of the world through Christ. Likewise we must look beyond the simple rebuilding of the earthly city of Zion to something far more enduring. New Testament writers assure us that this new Zion is the Church of the living God and also the New Jerusalem of Revelation 21/22. Entrance into this city is only possible because of the suffering and death of the Lord Jesus for us.

STUDY 7

THE FUTURE

QUESTIONS

DAY 1 *Isaiah 54:1-10?*
a) How does God illustrate the distress the nation has endured?
b) What would bring about a change in their fortunes?

DAY 2 *Isaiah 54:11-17.*
a) What does God promise the people of Jerusalem here?
b) How does this description of Jerusalem prefigure the New Jerusalem of Revelation 21:19-27?

DAY 3 *Isaiah 55:1-5.*
a) In the light of such verses as John 4:7-13; 6:35, what does this offer of water, wine and milk prefigure for us today?
b) What is emphasized in the first part of verse 3?

DAY 4 *Isaiah 55:6-13.*
a) What offer is extended to the people in verse 7. What conditions are attached to it?
b) Why is it we cannot always understand what happens to us?
c) What does God promise will always happen (v. 11)?

DAY 5 *Isaiah 56.*
a) What evidence is there that God's offer of salvation is universal and not just for Jews only?
b) How had the nation's rulers failed the people (vv. 9-12)?

DAY 6 *Isaiah 57:1-13.*
a) What reason is given for the premature death of good men? What did death mean for them? Compare this with Paul's attitude to death in Philippians 1:21, 23?
b) What was at the root of all the evils mentioned in verses 3-11?

DAY 7 *Isaiah 57:14-21.*
a) Pick out several verses which illustrate the condescending grace of the Almighty Eternal God.
b) In whom does God specially delight?
c) What distinguishes the wicked and righteous here?

NOTES

The prophet uses the analogy first of the childless widow and then of the rejected wife to show the sad state of Jerusalem during the exile. However this was now over. The childless woman would be so no more; the deserted wife would be taken back. The Almighty God would give Jerusalem back her children and would fully protect and instruct them. But there is more than just an earthly city in view (Gal. 4:26; compare also Isa. 54:11, 12 with Rev. 21:15-21). The call in Isaiah 54:2 is to a step of faith: to enlarge, lengthen and strengthen. Faith is 'being sure of what we hope for and certain of what we do not see' (Heb. 11:1). What is God saying to us today. He has often used the words of Isaiah 54:2 to call His people in every generation to a step of faith.

The opening words of Isaiah 55 may have been addressed to those who were still inclined to remain in Babylon where they had a certain amount of comfort and security despite lack of freedom. They are invited to a deeper satisfaction than Babylon can offer, and allied with this is the privilege of being God's ambassadors to all nations. True satisfaction is always found in what God offers. It is always on God's terms. Let us heed today the call to salvation through faith in the Lord Jesus. The theme of salvation for all nations continues to develop more fully in Isaiah 56 as the scene finally moves from Babylon to Jerusalem. All who wish to be God's people may be. It may seem odd to us that keeping the Sabbath is made a prerequisite for acceptance. However the Sabbath was God's sign from the beginning of Genesis and its keeping was a very good test for genuineness of profession, particularly for foreigners who had no such commitment. While there is merciful welcome for all sorts and conditions of people, by contrast God will still deal firmly with those of Israel who are supposed to lead and yet are more concerned with their own life of ease and luxury. In both the Old and New Testaments, bad religious leaders receive the strongest condemnation (Jer. 23:1-4; Ezek. 3:16-21; 33:1-17; 34; Matt. 15:1-14; 23:13-39).

God always makes a distinction between the good and the bad. In Isaiah 57, by far the greater part is taken up with a grim catalogue of evil that shows how Baal worship and idolatry continued to drag the people down – not least among those who had been left in Jerusalem (Ezek. 8). Again God throws out a challenge. Could idols save them? Once more he appeals to the people to trust Him. Once more He promises peace to those who are willing to be restored – but there is no peace for the wicked.

STUDY 8

THE TRUTH VERSUS THE FALSE

QUESTIONS

DAY 1 *Isaiah 58:1-9a.*
a) How had the people of Israel seen themselves?
b) What was wrong with their fasting? What more was needed?

DAY 2 *Isaiah 58: 9b-14.*
a) What is promised to those who honour God?
b) What special promise is made for those who put God first on the Sabbath (or any other day)?

DAY 3 *Isaiah 59:1-8.*
a) What serious consequence of sin is mentioned in verse 2?
b) What other consequences are mentioned, some in picturesque language?

DAY 4 *Isaiah 59:9-15a.*
a) What had inevitably followed their rebellion against God (vv. 8-11)?
b) What had the people (like David in Ps. 51:3, 4) begun to realize?

DAY 5 *Isaiah 59:15b-21.*
a) How do these verses confirm the statement of verse 1?
b) Ephesians 6:10-18; 1 Thessalonians 5:8. Why is the Christian to put on armour as God does here in Isaiah 59?

DAY 6 *Isaiah 60:1-14.*
a) What is the fundamental reason for the flow of the people towards Jerusalem? What did Jesus say would happen in Luke 13:29?
b) What indications are there that those coming were in earnest about their desire to worship?

DAY 7 *Isaiah 60:15-22.*
Which verses in particular show that the prophet has seen further than the simple reconstruction of an earthly city and has the heavenly Jerusalem of Revelation 21:22-27; 22:5 in mind?

'A lot of hypocrites!' Ever heard that muttered as an excuse for not going to church? Sadly, sometimes it is not without justification. One of the greatest stumbling blocks to people outside the Church is the sad fact that 'people's religion' is not always accompanied by simple goodness. The prophets in particular denounced this. God always expects kindness, love, mercy and justice in His people and any religious observance without these is useless. Paul says the same in I Corinthians 13 as does James in his letter (Jas. 1:26, 27; 2:14-17). A whole chapter (Matt. 23) is taken up with our Lord's condemnation of the same attitude among the Scribes and Pharisees. As with fasting so with the Sabbath. To set aside a day for God was not meant to be a burden but an opportunity for joy and fellowship.

Sin separates man from God (Isa. 59:2). All the rest of the grim catalogue of sin's effects on peoples' lives stems from this. The happy note behind it all is that God is not unwilling to hear and to help. So when people turn to Him in repentance as in Isaiah 59:12, they find God waiting and willing to intervene and bring them deliverance. The passage concludes with the far reaching promise, 'The Redeemer will come to Zion', and the prophet is assured of the certainty and endurance of the message that has come to him from God's Holy Spirit.

What a relief to come to chapter 60! A transition has been made from the shame of Israel's dereliction to a new glory. God has brought it about through His Redeemer. Now there is a magnificent procession of people coming to see the glory of God revealed in His City. Here we see Jerusalem rebuilt and entering upon its true vocation as a light to the nations around. Only in a very faint way was this prophecy fulfilled in the years following the return from exile.

As we see in Revelation 21:22, much of the language of Isaiah 60 seems to have more to do with the heavenly Jerusalem than the earthly one. This, of course, makes the whole chapter more relevant to us, since by faith we have 'come to Mount Zion and to the city of the living God, the heavenly Jerusalem' (Heb. 12:22). As we have noted before, the true Zion or Jerusalem, is not a city as such but stands for the people of God. For the New Testament, this people is the Church, the Bride of Christ.

STUDY 9

QUESTIONS

DAY 1 *Isaiah 61:1-3; Luke 4:16-21.*
a) After reading this passage from Isaiah, what did Jesus say about it?
b) Which statement in Isaiah 61:2 does the Lord Jesus apparently leave out deliberately from His message? Why (John 3:17)?

DAY 2 *Isaiah 61:4-11.*
a) Pick out some of the dramatic changes that will take place in the nation.
b) What kind of garments give true beauty and satisfaction (v. 10). For us, where do they come from (Rom. 3:22)?

DAY 3 *Isaiah 62:1-7.*
a) What burning desire is expressed for Jerusalem (v. 1)? What is God going to use to bring about this transformation (vv. 6, 7)?
b) God rejoices as a bridegroom (v. 5). How can these words be applied to the church (Eph. 5:22-27; Rev. 19:6-9; 21:9-11)?

DAY 4 *Isaiah 62:8-12.*
a) How does the Lord reassure the people concerning their future protection and provision?
b) What aspects of Isaiah's predictions in verses 10, 11 have been, or are being fulfilled today (Matt. 21:5)?

DAY 5 *Isaiah 63:1-6; Revelation 14:18-20.*
a) What is the dominant theme here?
b) What are the two outcomes of God's intervention?

DAY 6 *Isaiah 63:7-14.*
a) Before beginning his prayer in verse 15, what does the prophet do to prepare himself (Ps. 77:10-12)?
b) What is taught in this passage about the Person and Work of the Holy Spirit?

DAY 7 *Isaiah 63:15-19.*
a) Why does the prophet begin to pray?
b) On what grounds does he appeal to God for help (v. 16)?

NOTES

Again and again we see the two sides of the one coin in relation to the character of God: judgment or salvation.

In chapter 61 the prophet sees himself translated to the stricken city with a message of comfort and freedom, as well as a challenge for the people once more to be God's representative on earth. What an encouragement to those who were in the city and those who returned from Babylon. However our Lord Himself took the words of Isaiah 61:1, 2 and applied them to His own service on earth. So the message of this chapter becomes universal. It has been and will be a comfort and challenge for God's people for all time.

Shining through the call to prayer in Isaiah 62 is God's great longing for His people.

The pictures of the glory of God's people are varied and splendid: a crown, a royal diadem, a royal bride and finally the Holy People, the Redeemed of the Lord, Sought After and the City No Longer Deserted. It was a message calculated to fire the enthusiasm of those languishing in the ruined Jerusalem or in exile in Babylon. Undoubtedly many were inspired, among them, Ezra, Nehemiah, Zerubbabel and Zechariah. Again the promises are still valid, perhaps more so, for the readers of the New Testament, the worldwide people of God as the message goes to the ends of the earth, 'See, your Saviour comes' (Isa. 62:11).

The Day of the Lord was a Day of Hope for God's Old Testament people just as it is for the Church in the New Testament. But this Day is also a Day of Wrath for those who wilfully oppose God. In Isaiah 63, Edom with its similar ancestry and proximity to Israel, has less excuse for its bitter and continued opposition to the people of God. Yet Edom is only representative. The picture is applied in Revelation 19:11-21 to the King of Kings and Lord of Lords who finally destroys all opposition to His rightful reign and place. This Day of Vengeance is essential as part of the Day of Redemption for God's people. As long as there is rebellion there can be no peace. It is a principle still valid today.

Isaiah 63:7-19 is part of the prophet's prayer for the deliverance of Israel in her distress. The days of God's power with Moses are again recounted and this memory assures him that God can do it again, as He does not change. Note the plea of verse 16: 'you, O LORD, are our Father ...' No wonder this prophet had such supreme confidence!

STUDY 10

DELIGHT OR DESPAIR

QUESTIONS

DAY 1 *Isaiah 64:1-7.*
a) What was the prophet asking God to do?
b) What type of prayer does this section end with (I John 1:9)?

DAY 2 *Isaiah 64:8-12.*
a) On what grounds does the prophet continue to plead for God's intervention?
b) Are prayers like this still needed today?

DAY 3 *Isaiah 65:1-7; Romans 10:20, 21.*
a) Why could the people not blame God for their present plight?
b) What keeps people from finding God today?

DAY 4 *Isaiah 65:8-16.*
a) What does God promise for the future (v. 9)?
b) What two basic types of people are referred to here? What will be their contrasting?

DAY 5 *Isaiah 65:17-25; 2 Peter 3:10-13.*
a) How is the future shown to be better than anything they had ever experienced in the past?
b) Revelation 21:1-4. What impresses you most about this description of the future? Who can enjoy it (Rev. 21:27)?

DAY 6 *Isaiah 66:1-17.*
a) What promises are made concerning Jerusalem, the people of God?
b) What are the prospects of those who reject God?

DAY 7 *Isaiah 66:18-24.*
a) What is God's desire for the nations (v. 18)? How would this be achieved (vv. 18, 19)?
b) What fearful comparison is made between the righteous remnant and the rebellious majority to bring the prophecy to an end?

NOTES

Do we turn right or left? Will we go or stay? Choices are part of life. The same applies to spiritual things. But God in His goodness tells us clearly what results will come from what choices. The consequences are frightening for those who reject God. The choice is up to us.

The messages that God had given Isaiah for Israel had made a profound impression on the prophet himself and inspired him to pray in Isaiah 64. He remembers the past and calls on God to act as in days of old. He acknowledges that there is only one incomparable God. He reaffirms his belief that God acts for those who call on Him. At the same time he acknowledges his sin and the sin of his people. Even their righteousness is as filthy rags and they deserve nothing good from God. But God is their Father and they are totally in His hands. Although the prayer was for the prophet's own time and situation, so much of it can readily be taken upon the lips of God's people at any time. That means us! God has answered prayers like this in the past with revival blessing.

God answers the prayer of the prophet in Isaiah 65. He shows that the people of Jerusalem fall into two categories. The first are those who still rebel and choose idolatry and its attendant evils rather than the service of the true God. These will come under severe judgment. But there is a second group, the righteous remnant. These will be saved. In Isaiah 65:13-15 God's plans for His remnant are set in contrast against His judgments on the rebellious majority. For God's people on earth there is a marvellous promise: 'Before they call I will answer; while they are yet speaking I will hear' (Isa. 65:24).

When Solomon built the first temple in Jerusalem he acknowledged the truth of Isaiah 66:1, 'But will God really dwell on earth with men' (2 Chron. 6:18, see also Stephen's words in Acts 7:49). Isaiah 66:2 shows us clearly that God is concerned with the heart and man's attitude to Him rather than the outward signs of rebellion. Even so, the prophet returns to the realities of the return from exile and urges the people there to trust God to work with them and for them and to expect great things from Him. Once more (Isa. 66) a division is proclaimed. Those who still resist God and choose evil, God will punish fully and finally.

On the other hand, people of all nations will be gathered into Jerusalem so that His glory may be proclaimed among the nations. A foretaste of this was seen on the first Whit Sunday (Pentecost), Acts 2:5-12, 40, 44-47. Today Christians collectively from all over the world comprise God's temple (1 Cor. 3:16, 17; 1 Pet. 2:5). Similarly each individual Christian is the temple of God (1 Cor. 6:19). The glorious picture of the future (Rev. 21:22) is of the Lord God Almighty and the Lamb of God alone as His Temple and the Church as the New Jerusalem where God dwells for ever. Isaiah transports us from the ruins of Jerusalem and the bondage of Babylon into a glorious future. But characteristically the last word is with God and His warning of judgment on those who rebel.

ANSWER GUIDE

The following pages contain an Answer Guide. It is recommended that answers to the questions be attempted before turning to this guide. It is only a guide and the answers given should not be treated as exhaustive.

GUIDE TO STUDY 1

DAY 1
a) Their suffering was at an end and their sin paid for. Perhaps 'double' means that they had received ample punishment.
b) John the Baptist. He preached the necessity of repentance.
c) God had spoken it.

DAY 2
a) Their God was coming!
b) Man: mortal with a fleeting glory.
God: sovereign, powerful, eternal, yet gentle and kind.

DAY 3
a) That He is the Creator and all-powerful; He does not need any wisdom or help outside of Himself. His greatness we cannot fathom.
b) The might of Assyria and Babylon may appear awesome, but they are as nothing before God.

DAY 4
a) To creation (Ps. 19:1-4)). God not only created, He also sustains everything.
b) Idols are fabricated by human beings. They have even problems remaining upright! They cannot make the claims God makes.

DAY 5
a) It appeared as if God no longer knew about their problems or cared for them.
b) He reminds them who He is. It is impossible for Him to be in a position not to know or to help out.
c) Those who persevere in faith waiting upon God will receive supernatural strength (2 Cor. 12:9).

DAY 6
The Lord God.

DAY 7
a) They were not to fear or be dismayed because God was with them to strengthen and help them.
b) With fear and trembling. They were panicked into making more idols which obviously could not help as they had to be nailed down to prevent them toppling over!

GUIDE TO STUDY 2

DAY 1 a) Not to fear.
    b) Promises of Divine help and enabling and eventual victory.
    c) With great rejoicing in the Lord.

DAY 2 a) He promised an abundance of water, even in places where it might not be expected; also there was the abundance and variety of trees that would grow.
    b) God knows the end from the beginning. The future as well as the present is in His hands.

DAY 3 a) Their inability to answer the question of verse 22.
    b) Personal. Pharaoh and Nebuchadnezzar's dreams (Gen. 41:8, 16; Dan. 2:19).

DAY 4 God would be pleased with Him; His Spirit would be on Him; He would be gentle and humble, yet firm in His resolve; His mission would be universal.

DAY 5 a) He was the creator of everything.
    b) He is to be a light to the Gentiles; He will deliver those who are in the bondage of sin. (See Paul's commission, Acts 26:15-18.)

DAY 6 a) That of giving praise and glory to God.
    b) He is mighty and powerful and will triumph over His enemies, yet He is gentle and considerate to those who are weak and helpless.

DAY 7 a) Israel, God's servant, has been wilfully deaf and blind, paying no attention to God's commands.
    b) Because of their sin and deliberate rebellion, God has handed them over to suffer at the hands of their enemies.

GUIDE TO STUDY 3

DAY 1
a) They were reminded that they belonged to God, that He would be with them, to protect them and act on their behalf.
b) Jesus laid down His own life; His blood was shed for us.

DAY 2
a) Their deliverance would bear witness to the fact that what God had promised He was able to fulfil. This would be an eloquent witness to God's uniqueness and power (v. II).
b) The 'Ephesians' reference specifically refers to God's wisdom. God's love, grace, etc. could also be included as without which no one would be saved.

DAY 3
a) Their miraculous deliverance from Egypt under Moses.
To see God at work again in the life of the nation. He would act powerfully on their behalf, delivering them and providing for them even in very difficult situations (the desert).
b) God will blot out their transgressions and not remember their sins.

DAY 4
a) There would be a numerical increase and a willingness to be identified as belonging to God's people.
b) Personal. Many people became believers.

DAY 5
a) LORD, Lord Almighty, King, Redeemer, Rock, the first and last.
b) Ignorance; a rejection of the truth which leads to increasing blindness.

DAY 6
God's redemption and intervention on behalf of His people. What idols cannot do, He alone can do.

DAY 7
a) He has created and redeemed; He acts against false prophets and fulfils promises; He will restore the people to their own land.
b) Cyrus.

GUIDE TO STUDY 4

DAY 1   a) Subdue nations, remove barriers and open doors and make him rich. These promises remind us that nothing is impossible with God.
b) So that Israel would be released from captivity and that God would be glorified.

DAY 2   God is our Potter (Maker) and we are the clay. As Potter He knows what is best for us.

DAY 3   a) He will set Israel free and help rebuild Jerusalem.
b) There is only one God and that is the God of Israel.

DAY 4   a) To turn to God for salvation. There is no other Saviour but God.
b) Eventually everyone will submit (bow the knee) to God and confess that He alone is Lord.
Paul is speaking of an end time judgment.

DAY 5   a) Idols are burdensome, unable to hear or help and can be expensive to make; God upholds, sustains and carries those who believe in Him (even to old age!).
b) Despite fervent pleading, Baal did not respond to his prophets' request for help.

DAY 6   a) He is described as a bird of prey.
b) Personal. His ability to do what He promises is certainly emphasized.

DAY 7   a) She imagined herself eternal, unique and very wise.
b) They may attempt to predict but they cannot change the future They only increase problems (v. 13a) instead of solving them.

GUIDE TO STUDY 5

DAY 1   a) They would not listen to God's prophets despite the fulfilment of clear predictions.
b) It was a time of refining. Notice how God, for the honour of His own name, would not cut them off completely.

DAY 2   a) That God would use an 'ally' (Cyrus of Persia, v. 14) to defeat the Babylonians.
b) God teaches and gives peace and righteousness to those who listen and obey Him. The wicked have 'no peace' (v. 22).

DAY 3   a) The statement in verse 4 about the Servant's apparent failure. Jesus was rejected by His own people.
The Gentiles would have an opportunity to receive salvation (v. 6).
The Servant would be highly honoured (v. 7).
b) Called, prepared and protected Him (vv. 1, 2).

DAY 4   a) That of a guide (possibly a shepherd) and a mother.
b) Now is the day of salvation.

DAY 5   a) To show that the Gentiles would one day come to help God's people and would be their servants instead of oppressors.
b) It was due to judgment on them because of their sin.

DAY 6   a) Both help the weary, are obedient and both are mocked.
b) This reference in Isaiah is a prophetic reference to Jesus Christ.

DAY 7   a) God is with Him to help. Nothing can separate them from God's love and help.
b) The faithful fear, obey, trust and rely on God; the godless rely on their own 'light' and suffer as a consequence.

GUIDE TO STUDY 6

DAY 1 a) The fact that from one man and his wife Sarah, God had made the nation of Israel.
If God could make a nation from one couple, He was surely able to restore the nation to its former strength and glory.
b) Those who had God's law in their hearts. God's salvation that would last forever.

DAY 2 a) To act in power as He had done when they first come out of Egypt.
b) That they would return with great joy and celebration to Zion.

DAY 3 a) They were reminded that He created and was in control of everything. Their enemies were only mortal men. God reminded them that they were His people.
b) Personal. Proverbs 29:25; John 7:13; 12:42, 43, refer to the destructive influence of fear.

DAY 4 a) The drinking of the cup of God's wrath.
b) This cup was the symbol of Jesus taking upon Himself the sin of the world. Without His death there would have been no redemption for us.

DAY 5 a) God the Lord.
b) People need to hear about the Lord Jesus.
c) The need for purity. The need for holiness in the church and the warning against marrying unbelievers.

DAY 6 A picture of One who will suffer a lot and yet be highly exalted and adored.

DAY 7 a) Rejection (v. 3); smiting (v. 4); piercing (v. 5); wounds (v. 5). He bore them meekly, silently and willingly.
b) He was taking upon Him the punishment for our sins as He Himself was sinless.
c) Verse 10: He would see His offspring and his days would be prolonged.

GUIDE TO STUDY 7

DAY 1   a) They are compared to a widow, a deserted wife and a woman with no children.
b) God would no longer be angry with them and because of His great love and compassion for them would act on their behalf.

DAY 2   a) Prosperity, peace and protection.
b) Precious stones and jewels are used in its construction; the absence of evil and fear.

DAY 3   a) The salvation that God offers us in the Lord Jesus Christ. It is offered freely to all who come.
b) The importance of listening to and obeying God. God was offering what was essential to life and not just luxuries.

DAY 4   a) The offer of mercy and pardon. The need to forsake evil and turn to the Lord.
b) God's thoughts and ways are far beyond our understanding.
c) His Word will always be effective.

DAY 5   a) Foreigners and eunuchs, people technically excluded from the nation of Israel are now included among, and enjoy all the privileges of being part of God's people. Their acceptance is dependent on their obedience and not their background.
b) They had failed in their duties of being watchmen and shepherds.

DAY 6   a) To be spared from evil (calamity).
An entry into peace and rest. Paul recognized that death would be a stepping stone to something better, to being with Christ.
b) Idolatry.

DAY 7   a) Personal. Verses 15, 18 certainly illustrate it.
b) Those who are truly humble and contrite.
c) By the absence or possession of peace.

GUIDE TO STUDY 8

DAY 1 a) They expected help from God because of their religious practices. Fasting is mentioned here.
b) It was only mere ritual and not linked to any holy living. They needed to show compassion for the poor and oppressed in a practical way. Compare also these passages: Psalm 51:6, 16; Hosea 6:6; Amos 5:21-24; Micah 6:6-8; James 1:27.

DAY 2 a) Restoration, guidance protection and provision for all their needs.
b) Joy (v. 14).

DAY 3 a) It brings a separation between us and God.
b) Trouble, death, dissatisfaction and violence.

DAY 4 a) Injustice, blindness, weakness and sorrow.
b) That they had been sinning against God. God knew all about it.

DAY 5 a) God was clearly able to bring about deliverance for His people. (Notice that He was a well equipped warrior able to help them.)
b) Mainly as protection against the devil and evil spiritual forces.

DAY 6 a) The attractiveness of Jerusalem. People would realize that they need God's guidance and wisdom and see Jerusalem as the focal point where they can seek and find Him. People from all over the world would be in heaven.
b) They were bringing along expensive gifts.

DAY 7 Verses 19, 20 (this should warn us against taking the whole of the chapter literally, word for word.)

GUIDE TO STUDY 9

DAY 1   a) He claimed that these verses had been fulfilled by His coming.
b) He stopped just before, 'and the day of vengeance of our God'.
Personal. Perhaps because He was emphasizing the fact that He had come to save the world through the self-sacrificing of Himself.

DAY 2   a) No longer will the people be desolate, ashamed or sad.
b) The garments of salvation and righteousness. Through faith in the Lord Jesus.

DAY 3   a) That she be a city of righteousness, an example to the world of what God can do.
The prayers of His own people.
b) The church is the bride of Christ; the church is loved, changed and made holy by God.

DAY 4   a) With an oath guaranteed by His almighty power (v. 8).
b) The promised Saviour (Jesus) has come to Zion and a banner has been raised to the nations with the worldwide proclamation of the gospel message.

DAY 5   a) Judgment and the wrath of God.
b) Salvation for His people; destruction to the nations (John 5:24).

DAY 6   a) He looks back and recalls God's help in the past.
b) That He is a person who can be grieved (v. 10); He lives among God's people to guide and give rest (v. 14).

DAY 7   a) He is very concerned about the plight of the nation.
b) On the grounds that God was their Father and Redeemer; that God's sanctuary had been desecrated.

GUIDE TO STUDY 10

DAY 1   a) To reveal Himself in a powerful way among their enemies.
b) A confession of sin (especially v. 6).

DAY 2   a) On the grounds of their relationship to God (He was their Father and Creator) and the fact that the nation was in a mess.
b) Personal. There is an undoubted need for God to intervene in our nation.

DAY 3   a) They had been following idolatrous and probably occultic practices, and had been deliberately disobedient.
b) Personal.

DAY 4   a) The preservation of a righteous remnant among the people.
b) The righteous and wicked. Their contrasting destinies are described in verses 13, 14.

DAY 5   a) The pictures of long life, absence of war, no conflict in nature, etc. (Some interpret these verses as something that will happen literally on earth; others see in them a bright future which is filled out in more detail in the Christian's hope of heaven in the New Testament.)
b) Personal.
Only those whose names are in the Lamb's book of life, that is, born again Christians.

DAY 6   a) She will be a source of comfort and peace and be very rich.
b) Judgment, defeat and death.

DAY 7   a) That they would be aware of and see His glory.
God said that He would do it (v. 18). He would work through those who would go and proclaim it (v. 19) (Motyer in *The Prophecy of Isaiah* suggests the sign is a reference to the cross.)
b) The righteous will live for ever and serve God for ever; the wicked will be lost and suffer for ever. (Note the warning of Jesus in Mark 9:43-48.

THE WORD WORLDWIDE

We first heard of WORD WORLDWIDE over 20 years ago when Marie Dinnen, its founder, shared excitedly about the wonderful way ministry to one needy woman had exploded to touch many lives. It was great to see the Word of God being made central in the lives of thousands of men and women, then to witness the life-changing results of them applying the Word to their circumstances. Over the years the vision for WORD WORLDWIDE has not dimmed in the hearts of those who are involved in this ministry. God is still at work through His Word and in today's self-seeking society, the Word is even more relevant to those who desire true meaning and purpose in life. WORD WORLDWIDE is a ministry of WEC International, an interdenominational missionary society, whose sole purpose is to see Christ known, loved and worshipped by all, particularly those who have yet to hear of His wonderful name. This ministry is a vital part of our work and we warmly recommend the WORD WORLDWIDE 'Geared for Growth' Bible studies to you. We know that as you study His Word you will be enriched in your personal walk with Christ. It is our hope that as you are blessed through these studies, you will find opportunities to help others discover a personal relationship with Jesus. As a mission we would encourage you to work with us to make Christ known to the ends of the earth.

Stewart and Jean Moulds – British Directors, **WEC International**.

A full list of over 50 'Geared for Growth' studies can be obtained from:

ENGLAND *North East/South*: John and Ann Edwards
5 Louvaine Terrace, Hetton-le-Hole, Tyne & Wear, DH5 9PP
Tel. 0191 5262803 Email: rhysjohn.edwards@virgin.net
North West/Midlands: Anne Jenkins
2 Windermere Road, Carnforth, Lancs., LA5 9AR
Tel. 01524 734797 Email: anne@jenkins.abelgratis.com
West: Pam Riches Tel. 01594 834241

IRELAND Steffney Preston
33 Harcourts Hill, Portadown, Craigavon, N. Ireland, BT62 3RE
Tel. 028 3833 7844 Email: sa.preston@talk21.com

SCOTLAND Margaret Halliday
10 Douglas Drive, Newton Mearns, Glasgow, G77 6HR
Tel. 0141 639 8695 Email: mhalliday@onetel.net.uk

WALES William and Eirian Edwards
Penlan Uchaf, Carmarthen Road, Kidwelly, Carms., SA17 5AF
Tel. 01554 890423 Email: penlanuchaf@fwi.co.uk

UK CO-ORDINATOR

Anne Jenkins
2 Windermere Road, Carnforth, Lancs., LA5 9AR
Tel. 01524 734797 Email: anne@jenkins.abelgratis.com

UK Website: www.gearedforgrowth.co.uk